D0056082

hide
this
french
book
for lovers

Berlitz Publishing
New York   Munich   Singapore

Hide This French Book for Lovers

Contacting the Editors
Every effort has been made to provide accurate information in this publication, but changes are inevitable. The publisher cannot be responsible for any resulting loss, inconvenience or injury. We would appreciate it if readers would call our attention to any errors or outdated information by contacting Berlitz Publishing, 193 Morris Avenue, Springfield, NJ 07081, USA. email: comments@berlitzbooks.com

Second Printing: February 2007
Printed in China

Writer: Claire Caro
Publishing Director: Sheryl Olinsky Borg
Senior Editor/Project Manager: Lorraine Sova
Editor: Emily Bernath
Cover and Interior Design: Wee Design Group, Blair Swick
Production Manager: Elizabeth Gaynor
Illustrations: Kyle Webster, Amy Zaleski

Hide This French Book *for lovers* has everything from cheesy pick-up lines to erotic sex talk. "Hot" words are labeled with ▮ and the hottest language with ▮. Go ahead—get hot 'n heavy with French.

NOTE: You get to make some cool nasal sounds when speaking French. In the phonetics, they're noted as (vowel) + N. Don't pronounce that "N" strongly; it's there to show the nasal quality of the previous vowel. Make that nasal sound by pronouncing the vowel through the mouth and the nose—at the same time. Fun!

table of contents

Vous venez souvent ici?

voo vuh-nay soo-vahN ee-see

Come here often?

It sounds better in French.

Vous n'êtes pas du coin?

voo net pah dew kwaN

hooking up

Do you live around here?

Literally: You're not from around here?

hooking up

Je ne vous ai pas déjà vu 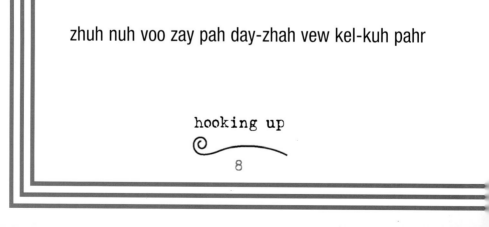/ vue quelque part?

zhuh nuh voo zay pah day-zhah vew kel-kuh pahr

I've seen you somewhere. Have we met before?

Having a "déjà vu"?!

Vous attendez quelqu'un?

voo zah-tahN-day kel-kaN

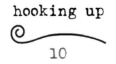

hooking up

10

Are you waiting for someone?

If the answer is "no", make your move.

hooking up

Je peux vous inviter à prendre un verre?

zhuh puh voo zaN-vee-tay ah prahN-druh aN vair

Can I buy you a drink?

A typical line—but it works every time.

hooking up

13

Cette place est prise?

set plahss eh preez

Is that seat taken?

Get close to him or her!

hooking up

Est-ce que vous avez du feu?

es-kuh voo zah-vay dew fuh

hooking up

16

Do you have a light?

Spark up a conversation.

Pourriez-vous m'aider, je suis perdu♂/ perdue♀?

poor-ee-ay voo meh-day zhuh swee pair-dew

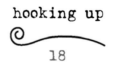

hooking up

18

Could you help me? I'm lost.

Perhaps he or she will take you there personally.

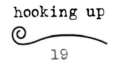

Vous êtes charmant ♂/ charmante ♀.

voo zet shah-mahN/shah-mahNt

You're charming.

Flattery will get you somewhere!

hooking up

21

Il/Elle me fait fondre.

eel/el muh fay fohN-druh

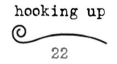

He/She makes me melt.

Feeling warm and fuzzy?

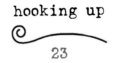

hooking up

Il/Elle me fait craquer.

eel/el muh fay krah-kay

hooking up

24

He/She's gorgeous.

Literally: He/She makes me crunch.

hooking up

Regarde-moi cette bombe!

ruh-gahd-mwah set bohNb

hooking up

Look at that sex bomb!

hooking up

the scoop

The population of available singles in France is at an all-time high. That means that men *and* women are actively trying to attract the opposite sex. The French often make their first approach with eye contact; if the person you're interested in acknowledges you, go ahead and approach him or her—but, practice your pick-up line before making that first move!

Embrasse-moi.

ahN-brahss-mwah

kisses & hugs

Kiss me.

Ah, instant gratification...

Fais-moi un câlin.

fay-mwah aN kah-laN

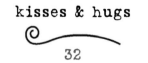

kisses & hugs

32

Give me a hug.

Get cozy.

kisses & hugs

33

Je suis tout excité♂.

Je suis toute excitée♀.

zhuh swee toot ex-ee-tay

kisses & hugs

34

I'm horny.

Literally: I'm all excited.

J'ai envie de toi.

zhay ahN-vee duh twah

I want you now.

Don't waste any time.

kisses & hugs

Fais-moi l'*amour*.

fay-mwah lah-moor

Make *love* to me.

A romantic way to say it.

kisses & hugs

Je ne veux pas d'une relation exclusive.

zhuh nuh vuh pah dewn ruh-lah-see-ohN ex-klew-seev

kisses & hugs

40

I'm not into exclusive relationships.

Prefer not to be monogamous?

kisses & hugs

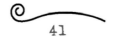

41

C'est un ami-câlin .

set aN nah-mee-kah-laN

C'est une amie-câlin ♀.

set ewn nah-mee-kah-laN

kisses & hugs

42

We're friends
with benefits.

The best of both worlds…

kisses & hugs

On sort ensemble.

ohN saw ahN-sahN-bluh

We're dating.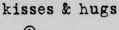

Serious stuff, huh?

kisses & hugs

He's my boyfriend.
She's my girlfriend.

*Nix the word "petit ♂/petite ♀"
if you wanna sound really French.*

kisses & hugs

47

Je l'aime à la folie.

zhuh lem ah lah foh-lee

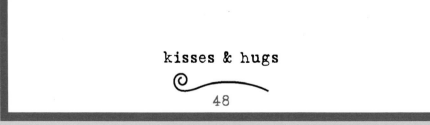

kisses & hugs

48

I'm so in *love* with him/her.

Literally: I love him/her to be mad.

Nous sommes fous l'un de l'autre.

noo sum foo
laN duh loh-truh

kisses & hugs

50

We're crazy about each other.

Lucky you!

kisses & hugs

51

kisses & hugs

52

the scoop

French people are quite physical, so don't be shocked if, when you meet someone for the first time, he or she gives you a kiss on both cheeks. This isn't a come-on, it's just a French greeting. You get—and give—two kisses (one on each cheek) in most French towns, three in the south of France, and four in the north. Just follow the love!

kisses & hugs

J'ai flirté avec lui.

zhay fluh-tay ah-vek lwee

love & sex

54

I made out with him.

The French word "flirter"

means a bit more than

just flirting in this context.

Tu sais à quoi je pense, là tout de suite?

tew say ah kwah zhuh pahNs lah toot sweet

56

Do you know what I'm thinking about right now?

Think dirty.

love & sex

57

Rejoins-moi
dans la chambre.

ruh-zhwaN-mwah dahN lah shahN-bruh

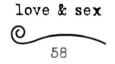

love & sex

Follow me
to the bedroom.

You're not tired, are you?!

love & sex

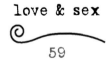

Un petit massage?

aN puh-tee mahs-sahzh

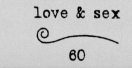

(Can I give you)
a little massage?

Who would say no?

love & sex

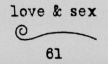

Je suis tout ♂/ toute ♀ à toi.

zhuh swee toot ah twah

love & sex

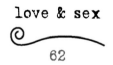

I'm all yours.

Yeah, baby.

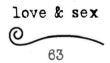

Déshabille-moi.

day-zah-bee-mwah

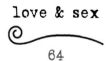

love & sex

Take off my clothes.

It's the name of a very popular French song.

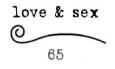

love & sex

Prends-moi maintenant.

prahN-mwah maN-tuh-nahN

love & sex

Take me now.

*You know what
this means!*

Fais de moi ta chose.

fay duh mwah tah shohz

I'm your plaything.

Whatever puts you in the mood.

love & sex

Tu aimes ça?

tew em sah

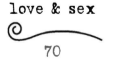

love & sex

Do you like this?

So, does that feel good?

love & sex

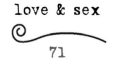

71

Tu es une petite cochonne.

tew eh ewn puh-teet koh-shun

You are a little pig.

You're dirty!

love & sex

Un plan cul, ça te tente?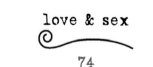

aN plahN kew sah tuh tahNt

love & sex

Are you interested in a great @#&!?

This can be very rude.

On se mate
un film porno?

ohN suh maht aN feelm paw-noh

love & sex

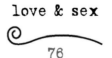

76

Wanna watch a porno?

You need to do something

to pass the time!

love & sex

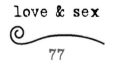

Tu as des préservatifs?

tew ah day pray-sair-vah-teef

love & sex

78

Do you have condoms?

That's a forward question, isn't it?

love & sex

Quels sont tes fantasmes?

kel sohN tay fahN-tahz-muh

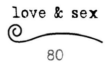

love & sex

What are your (sexual) fantasies?

Go ahead—share.

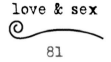

love & sex

81

Nous avons couché ensemble.

noo zah-vohN koo-shay ahN-sahN-bluh

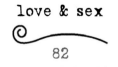

love & sex

82

We slept together.

Doubt anyone slept!

love & sex

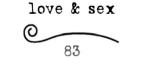

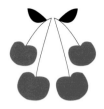

Nous avons passé
la nuit ensemble.

noo zah-vohN pahs-say lah nwee ahN-sahN-bluh

love & sex

We spent
the night together.

Doing...?

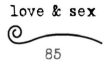
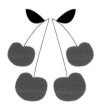

Nous avons baisé toute la nuit.

noo zah-vohN bay-zay toot lah nwee

We @#&!ed all night.

Really?!

love & sex

love & sex

the scoop

Talking about sex isn't taboo in France. Whether you want to bring up the topic of foreplay—a must for just about any French person—sex, or sexual fantasies, feel free to talk openly about your interests with your partner. Even doctors talk frankly about sex; articles recently published in French medical journals recommend sex three to four times a week. So go ahead and have some fun!

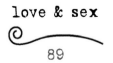

love & sex

Je t'*aime*.

zhuh tem

u + me 4ever

I *love* you.

Be honest about your feelings.

u + me 4ever

J'aime tout chez toi.

zhem too shay twah

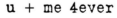 u + me 4ever

92

I love everything about you.

Give him or her an ego boost.

u + me 4ever

93

Tu es à tomber.

tew eh ah tohN-bay

u + me 4ever

★ ★ ★ ★ ★ ★ ★ ★ ★

You're hot.

Literally: You're to fall for.

★ ★ ★ ★ ★ ★ ★ ★ ★

u + me 4ever

On a eu du bon temps.

ohN ah ew dew bohN tahN

u + me 4ever

We had a great time together.

Want the relationship to continue?

u + me 4ever

Appelle-moi.

ah-pel-mwah

u + me 4ever

98

Call me.

*Cross your fingers that
he or she does.*

u + me 4ever

On peut se revoir?

ohN puh suh ruh-vwah

u + me 4ever

100

Can I see you again?

When and where, baby?

u + me 4ever

101

Je ne peux plus
me passer de toi.

zhuh nuh puh plew muh pahs-say duh twah

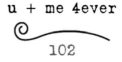

u + me 4ever

102

I can't live without you.

You're obsessed!

u + me 4ever

Viens vivre avec moi.

vyaN vee-vruh ah-vek mwah

u + me 4ever

104

Move in with me.

Pack your bags and go!

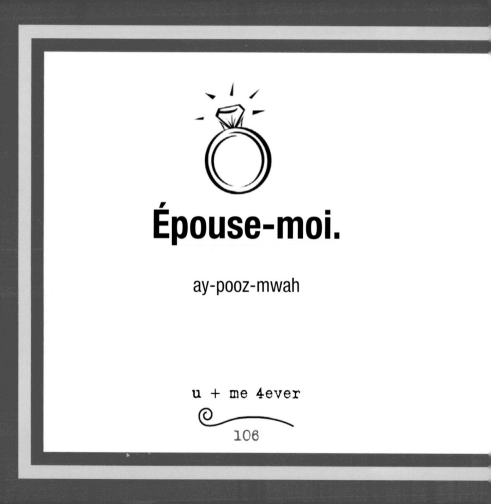

Épouse-moi.

ay-pooz-mwah

u + me 4ever

106

Marry me.

Where's the ring?!

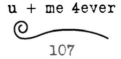

u + me 4ever

107

Je suis enceinte.

zhuh swee ahN-saNt

I'm pregnant.

Ah, family...

u + me 4ever

110

The trend nowadays is for French couples to live together monogamously, without going through the hooplah of a wedding. Some also decide on signing PACS, Civil Pact of Solidarity, which is a civil contract that binds the couple legally. It ensures all the benefits of marriage and eliminates the disadvantages, namely, divorce. Welcome to a new world!

mon amour

mohN ah-moor

mon cœur

mohN kuhr

sweet talk

my love
my heart

*Use these with someone
you completely adore.*

mon bébé

mohN bay-bay

my baby

For the one you'll always love...

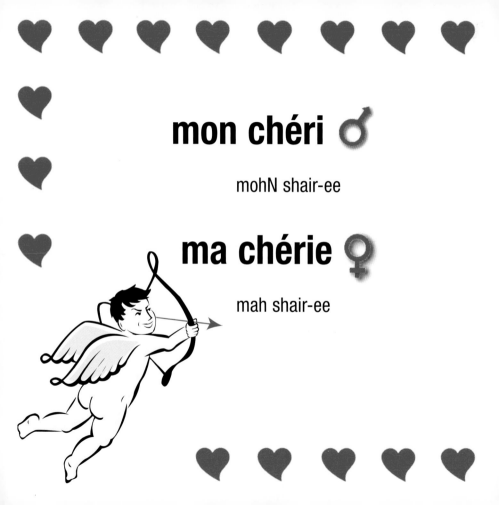

my dear

How sweet!

 **ma petite puce**

mah puh-teet pewss

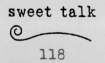

sweet talk

118

my little one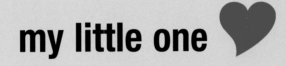

Literally: my little flea

mon poussin

mohN poo-saN

mon canard

mohN kah-nah

my pet

Literally: my chick

Literally: my duck

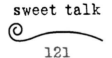

mon ange

mohN nahnzh

my angel

Just heavenly...

sweet talk

Restons bons amis.

res-tohN bohN zah-mee

breaking up

124

Let's just be friends.

A classy way to end it.

breaking up

C'est fini entre nous.

say fee-nee ahN-truh noo

breaking up